PIANO | VOCAL | GUITAR

RED HOT CHILI PEPPERS
GRE

ISBN-13: 978-1-4234-1999-0
ISBN-10: 1-4234-1999-5

7777 W. BLUEMOUND RD. P.O. BOX 13819 MILWAUKEE, WI 53213

In Australia Contact:
Hal Leonard Australia Pty. Ltd.
4 Lentara Court
Cheltenham, Victoria, 3192 Australia
Email: ausadmin@halleonard.com

Visit Hal Leonard Online at
www.halleonard.com

CONTENTS

4 Under the Bridge

9 Give It Away

22 Californication

32 Scar Tissue

44 Soul to Squeeze

50 Otherside

37 Suck My Kiss

56 By the Way

65 Parallel Universe

70 Breaking the Girl

82 My Friends

86 Higher Ground

75 Universally Speaking

106 Road Trippin'

92 Fortune Faded

98 Save the Population

UNDER THE BRIDGE

Words and Music by ANTHONY KIEDIS, FLEA,
JOHN FRUSCIANTE and CHAD SMITH

GIVE IT AWAY

Words and Music by ANTHONY KIEDIS, FLEA,
JOHN FRUSCIANTE and CHAD SMITH

Give it a-way now.

Give it a-way now.

Give it a-way now.

Give it a-way now.

Give it a-way now.

Give it a-way now.

Give it a-way.

CALIFORNICATION

Words and Music by ANTHONY KIEDIS, FLEA,
JOHN FRUSCIANTE and CHAD SMITH

SCAR TISSUE

Words and Music by ANTHONY KIEDIS, FLEA,
JOHN FRUSCIANTE and CHAD SMITH

(1., 3.) Scar tis-sue that I wish you saw. __ Sar - cas-tic mis-ter-know-it - all. __
(2.) Blood loss in a bath-room stall, __ South-ern girl with a scar-let drawl. __

Close your eyes and I'll __ kiss you 'cause __ with the birds I'll share. __
Wave good-bye to Ma __ and Pa 'cause __ with the birds I'll share. __

With the birds I'll share this lone - ly ___ view. ___ And

with the birds I'll share this lone - ly ___ view. ___ And

To Coda ⊕

Push me up a-gainst the wall, _ young Ken-tuck-y girl in a push-up bra. ___
Soft spo-ken with a bro-ken jaw, _ step out-side, but not to brawl. _

Fall - in' all o - ver my-self to lick ___ your heart and taste _ your health. 'Cause
Au-tumn's sweet, we call it fall. I'll make it to the moon if I have to crawl. And

- ly   new. _____

With the birds I'll   share   this   lone - ly   view. _____

SUCK MY KISS

Words and Music by ANTHONY KIEDIS, FLEA,
JOHN FRUSCIANTE and CHAD SMITH

Yeah.

Oh yeah.

(2nd time only)

(Hit me!)

Should have been could have been would have been dead if I

SOUL TO SQUEEZE

from the Paramount Motion Picture THE CONEHEADS

Words and Music by ANTHONY KIEDIS, FLEA,
JOHN FRUSCIANTE and CHAD SMITH

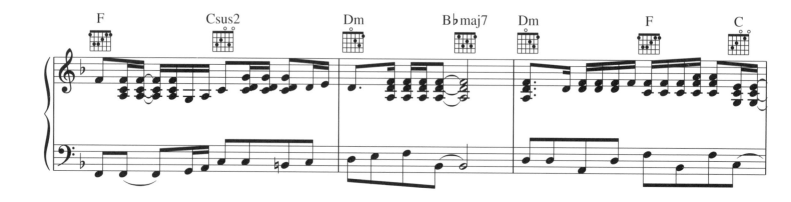

OTHERSIDE

Words and Music by ANTHONY KIEDIS, FLEA,
JOHN FRUSCIANTE and CHAD SMITH

How long, — how long _____ will I slide?

Sep - a - rate my side. _____ I don't, __

__ I don't be - lieve it's bad. _____

BY THE WAY

Words and Music by ANTHONY KIEDIS, FLEA,
JOHN FRUSCIANTE and CHAD SMITH

To Coda ⊕

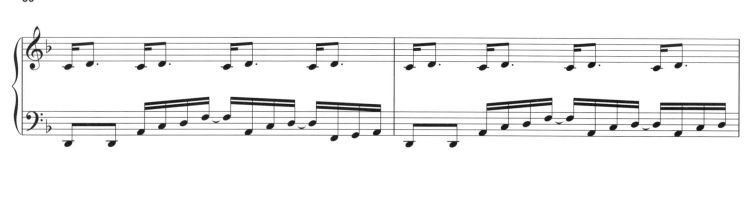

D.S. al Coda

CODA

F5

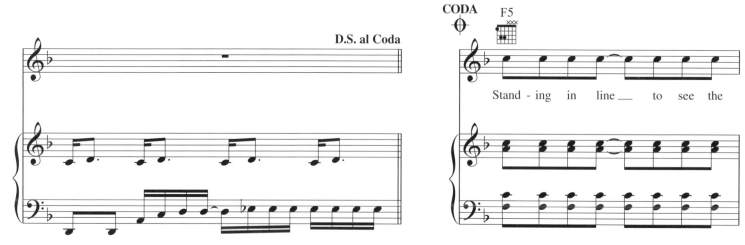

Stand - ing in line ___ to see the

C   A5

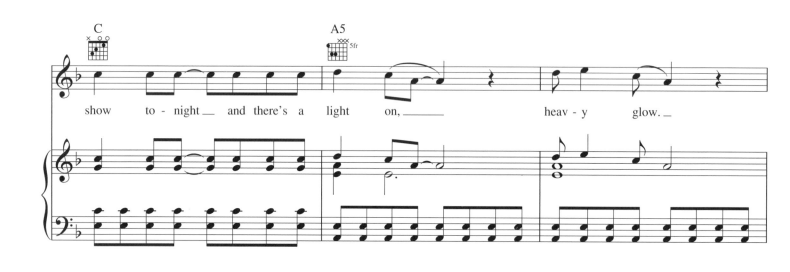

show to - night ___ and there's a light on, _____ heav - y glow. __

F5   C5   A5

By the way ___ I ____ tried to say ___ I'd be ___ there

Ooh, aah, kiss ya' then I miss ya'. Ooh, aah, kiss ya' then I miss ya'.

Ooh, aah, kiss ya' then I miss ya'. Ooh, aah, kiss ya' then I miss ya'.

Ooh, aah.

Stand - ing in line ___ to see the

PARALLEL UNIVERSE

Words and Music by ANTHONY KIEDIS,
FLEA, JOHN FRUSCIANTE and CHAD SMITH

*Accompaniment is played as 16th notes on recorded version.

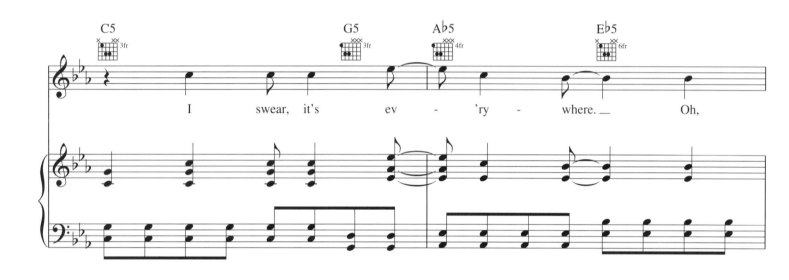

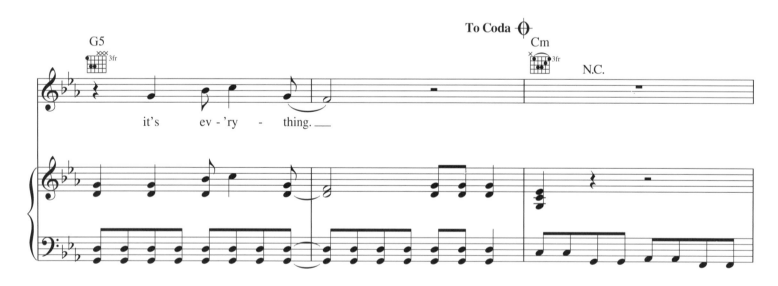

D.S. al Coda

CODA

Guitar solo ad lib. to end

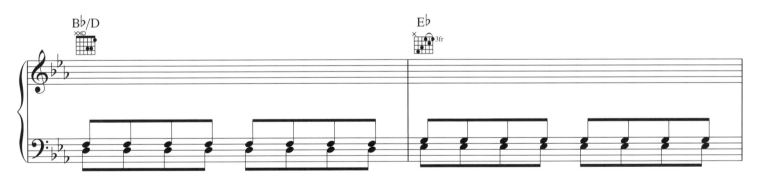

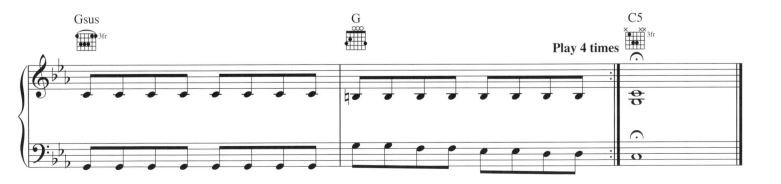

BREAKING THE GIRL

Words and Music by ANTHONY KIEDIS, FLEA,
JOHN FRUSCIANTE and CHAD SMITH

CODA

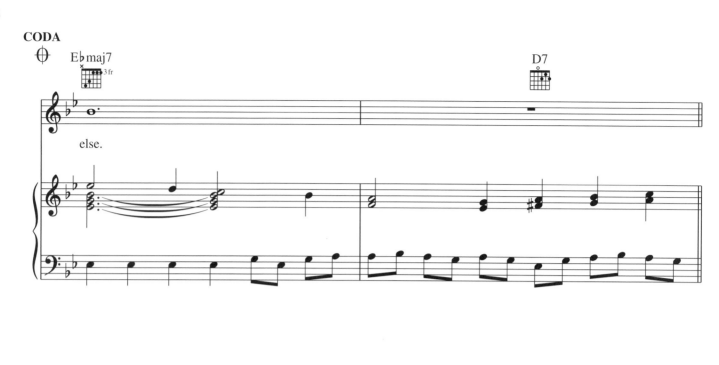

else.

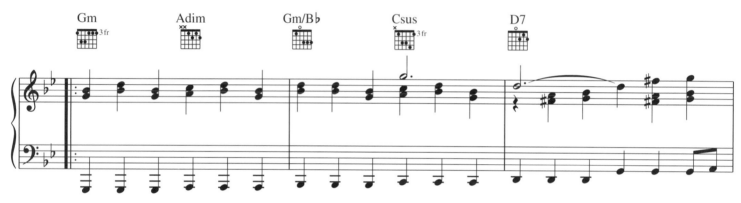

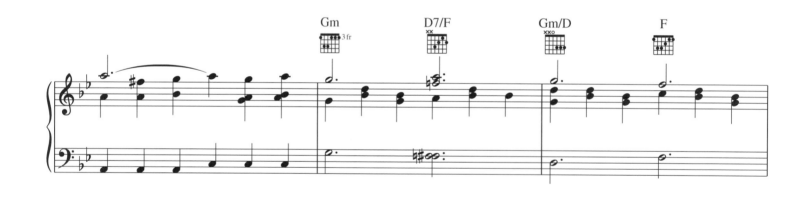

Repeat and Fade   **Optional Ending**

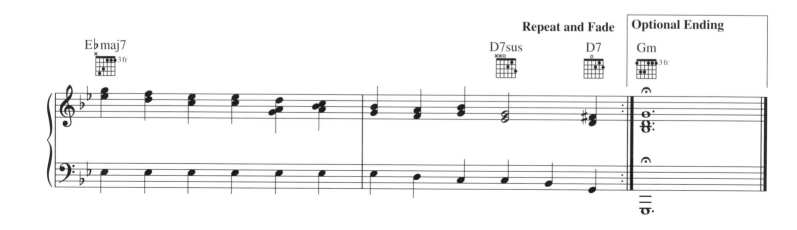

UNIVERSALLY SPEAKING

Words and Music by ANTHONY KIEDIS,
FLEA, JOHN FRUSCIANTE and CHAD SMITH

saw your face, _____ el - e - gant _ and tired, _

Sil - ver - et - ta the jets ____ of a life - time.

MY FRIENDS

Words and Music by ANTHONY KIEDIS, FLEA,
CHAD SMITH and DAVID NAVARRO

HIGHER GROUND

Words and Music by
STEVIE WONDER

Fast Bluesy Rock

Peo - ple _____ keep on _____
pow - ers _____ keep on _____
teach - ers _____ keep on _____
lov - ers _____ keep on _____

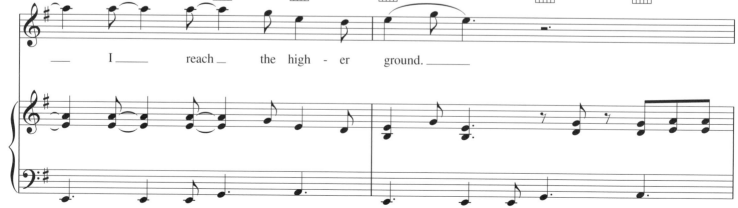

FORTUNE FADED

Words and Music by ANTHONY KIEDIS,
FLEA, JOHN FRUSCIANTE and CHAD SMITH

Bright Funk Rock

A
G
B5
ev - 'ry time I lose
al - ti - tude.
1
D
A
G
2, 3
D
A
G
A6
D
A
G
So di - vine,
hell of an el - e - va - tor.
Bm
F♯5
Bm/D
A6
D
A
All the while, my for - tune fad - ed.
Nev - er mind

Come on, God, _ do I _____ seem bul - let - proof? _

SAVE THE POPULATION

Words and Music by ANTHONY KIEDIS,
FLEA, JOHN FRUSCIANTE and CHAD SMITH

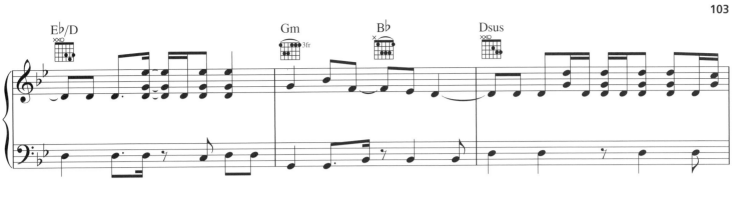

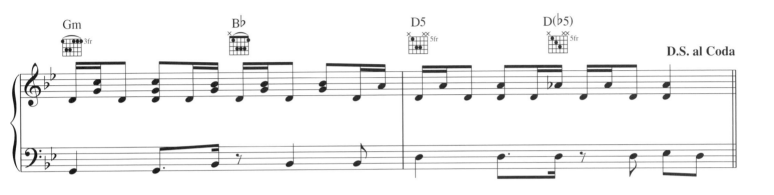

D.S. al Coda

CODA

Stay all night, __ we'll save __ the pop - u - la - tion. (Stay all night, __ we'll save __

__ the pop - u - la - tion.)

Stay all night, __ we'll save __ the pop - u - la -

ROAD TRIPPIN'

Words and Music by ANTHONY KIEDIS,
FLEA, JOHN FRUSCIANTE and CHAD SMITH

These smil - ing eyes _ are just a mir - ror for. _

Your smil - ing eyes _ are just a mir - ror for. _

Play 3 times

rall. on 3rd time